Created especially for

_____

Love from

_____

Cherish [verb]: protect and care for (someone) lovingly;
hold (something) dear; keep (a hope or ambition) in one's mind.

ABOUT THE AUTHOR

Shaela Mauger and Harpermartin

Born and raised in Wagga Wagga regional New South Wales, Shaela has pursued her love of graphic design through university and began her career as a designer for a local printer.

Since becoming a mother, Shaela has fine tuned her passion for design towards what's most important to her: loved ones, and cherishing the time we have with them. Now, after half a decade of having her own design business, Shaela has launched Harpermartin — paying homage to her parents' family names — and this series of keepsake books, created to celebrate life and love in all its forms.

The series is available at www.harpermartin.com.au

ISBN 978-0-6482778-1-1

Cherish

a book about us

By Shaela Mauger

Table of Contents

In memory of my Dad, Greg x

PREFACE

Life is so precious and how long we have to enjoy it is a true unknown.

This book was created as a result of my own life experiences. I lost my Dad when I was five years old. Being so young, I don't remember a lot of the time I had with him, but what I do have is a letter which he wrote me before his passing. I cherish this gift and find solace in his words.

Now, with children of my own, the weight of his absence has resurfaced. When I created this book, I conjured all of the things that would have comforted me. The prompts included within will hopefully inspire all that you want to tell your loved ones. The book is divided into two sections, the first part tells the story of the person writing it, the second captures the special relationship between the person writing it and the recipient.

We live in the digital age, but there is something truly special about the handwritten text, the uniqueness and beauty of a person's handwriting and the ebb and flow of their words. Each photo tells a different story and evokes a beautiful memory. This book is a tangible tether that, while never replacing the person who wrote it, can provide untold consolation to the recipient at different times in their life.

Consider this book a great big bear hug, the tight squeeze, the call of encouragement, the quiet moment of reflection from the one you love.

With love,

Shaela xx

Founder, Harpermartin

My Story

This is the story of my life to date.
It includes everything that makes me who I am today
and my hopes and dreams for the future.

My Story...

Full name:

_____

Nickname:

_____

Date of birth:

_____

Born at:

_____

Weight and length at birth:

_____

Parents:

_____

Grandparents:

_____

_____

Siblings:

_____

_____

_____

Schooling and higher education:

_____

_____

_____

_____

_____

_____

I worked for:

_____

_____

_____

_____

_____

Clubs I was involved in:

_____

_____

_____

_____

My greatest achievement:

_____

_____

_____

_____

_____

My favourite childhood memories:

_____

_____

_____

_____

_____

_____

_____

_____

_____

My first love:

_____

_____

_____

_____

My biggest regret:

_____

_____

_____

_____

_____

_____

_____

Highlights of my life and moments that I treasure:

_____

_____

_____

_____

_____

_____

_____

My favourite...

Songs:

Hobbies:

Teams:

Lucky number:

Colour:

My favourite holiday

This is my bucket list that I want you to see,
can you fill in the gaps if not completed by me x

	Challenge	Completion date	✓
1			
2			
3			
4			
5			
6			
7			
8			
9			
10			

My hopes and dreams

My favourite quote to live by...

_____

_____

_____

_____

_____

Our Story

This is all about our special journey together in this world.
It captures everything I love about you from the day you came
into my life and my wishes for you in the future.

A letter to you

_____

_____

_____

_____

_____

_____

_____

_____

_____

_____

_____

_____

_____

_____

My dreams and wishes for you:

My nickname for you:

_____

_____

_____

_____

I was so proud of you when…:

_____

_____

_____

_____

_____

_____

_____

_____

Remember when:

Thank you for...:

1:

_____

_____

_____

2:

_____

_____

_____

3:

_____

_____

_____

4:

_____

_____

_____

5:

_____

_____

_____

6:

_____

_____

_____

7:

_____

_____

_____

8:

_____

_____

_____

9:

_____

_____

_____

10:

_____

_____

_____

I love you to the moon and back
and more than all the stars in the sky

www.ingramcontent.com/pod-product-compliance
Lightning Source LLC
Chambersburg PA
CBHW040257100426
42811CB00011B/1299